The Best Christmas Pageant Ever

Barbara Robinson

AF207649

STUDENT PACKET

NOTE:

The trade book edition of the novel used to prepare this guide is
found in the Novel Units catalog and on the Novel Units website.
Using other editions may have varied page references.

Please note: We have assigned Interest Levels based on our
knowledge of the themes and ideas of the books included in the
Novel Units sets, however, please assess the appropriateness of this
novel or trade book for the age level and maturity of your students
prior to reading with them. You know your students best!

BN 978-1-56137-701-5

To order, contact your
local school supply store, or:

Toll-Free Fax: 877.716.7272
Phone: 888.650.4224
3901 Union Blvd., Suite 155
St. Louis, MO 63115

sales@novelunits.com

novelunits.com

Activity: To read for information

Special Trees

Originally, the trees used by many families in their homes in December came from the forest. Nowadays, most evergreen trees used for this purpose are plantation-grown.

Plantation trees are grown in cultivated plots, sheared and cared for in order to provide consumers with the best possible trees.

These trees usually begin life in a nursery where superior seeds are planted and grown to two-year-old seedlings. The seedlings are taken from the nursery beds and replanted. It takes constant and skilled care over several years for an evergreen tree to get a healthy start.

While growing, the trees serve as wildlife habitats, they increase soil stability and provide a pleasant looking environment for people. However, during the five to sixteen years that these trees are growing into well-shaped 6-to-8 foot marketable trees, they face many hazards. There can be too much or not enough rain and/or sunshine, and insects or disease may attack. They also may be stolen by tree thieves.

Fall is the time for the tree harvest. The best trees are cut down, bundled with twine for transporting, and trucked around the country, to be sold and then enjoyed by many. Even after the holidays, evergreen trees are useful. They make good backyard bird feeders, the branches make good mulch for a garden, and the trunks can be cut into firewood.

Read the following statements. Mark each either T (True) or F (False).

_____ 1. Most evergreen trees used for decorating homes in December are plantation grown.
_____ 2. Plantation trees do not require a great deal of care.
_____ 3. The trees are useful as wildlife habitats while they are growing.
_____ 4. These trees take from five to sixteen years to be ready for market.
_____ 5. Thieves do not steal trees.
_____ 6. Fall is the time for the tree harvest.

Source for Information: National Christmas Tree Association.

Activity: To use organizational skills

Saturday

"After all, it was a Saturday, and not much going on." (page 1)

The Herdmans set fire to Fred Shoemaker's toolhouse on a Saturday while playing with a chemistry set that Leroy had stolen from the hardware store.

What do you do on Saturday? Write down your schedule for a typical Saturday. Give complete details, including the times, places, activities, companions, etc.

_____

_____

_____

_____

_____

_____

_____

_____

_____

_____

_____

_____

_____

_____

_____

Activity: To use mathematics skills

Doughnuts

"It was a terrific fire—two engines and two police cars and all the volunteer firemen and five dozen doughnuts sent up from the Tasti-Lunch Diner. The doughnuts were supposed to be for the firemen, but by the time they got the fire out the doughnuts were all gone. The Herdmans got them..."
(page 2)

1. How many doughnuts would each of the six Herdman children get, if they were divided equally?

2. Do some doughnut price comparisons. Add your information to the chart that has been started. Use the information that you have to calculate the missing figures. Round up to the nearest cent.

Brand Name or Bakery Name	Number of Doughnuts	Cost	Cost Each	Cost per Dozen
Jewel	1	39 cents	_____	_____
Seven-Eleven	10	$2.89	_____	_____
Dunkin' Donuts	1	49 cents	_____	_____
Patisserie	6	$6.99	_____	_____
Cake Box	1	65 cents	_____	_____
_____	_____	_____	_____	_____
_____	_____	_____	_____	_____
_____	_____	_____	_____	_____
_____	_____	_____	_____	_____

What kind of doughnut do you like the best? _____

Activity: To make a poster

The Cat

There was also a sign in the yard that said "Beware Of The Cat." (page 4)

The Herdmans' cat is described on pages 4 and 5. The sign in the yard, "Beware Of The Cat," may not be enough to warn someone who did not know the Herdmans.

Make a poster that could be placed in the yard that gives more of a warning about the cat.

Materials needed: cardboard from a box or shirt cardboard, crayons or markers

Make an illustration of the poster in the space below.

Activity: To use imagination to put a scene into cartoon form

The Cat At School

"One day Claude Herdman emptied the whole first grade in three minutes flat when he took the cat to Show-and-Tell." (page 5)

Reread the description of the cat at school, pages 5 and 7. Draw a cartoon of one incident, and give the thoughts of the cat at that moment in time. Write a caption for the cartoon.

A CATastrophe At School

Activity: To write a limerick

The Cat, Continued

" 'I don't think it's a regular cat at all,' " the mailman told my father. 'I think those kids went up in the hills and caught themselves a bobcat.' " (page 4)

A **limerick** is a five-line poem. The first, second and fifth lines rhyme. The third and fourth lines rhyme. The fifth line of a limerick is often written with a humorous twist.

Write a limerick about the unusual cat that belongs to the Herdmans.

For example:

My Limerick

The Herdmans have an unusual cat;
There's none that is meaner than that.
It has one eye and a broken tail;
It chases after the man with the mail,
And any kid swinging a bat.

Your Limerick

_____ 1

_____ 2

_____ 3

_____ 4

_____ 5

Name_____

Activity: To use visual perceptual skills

Tangram Cat

"Now and then you'd see Mrs. Herdman, walking the cat on a length of chain around the block. But she worked double shifts at the shoe factory, and wasn't home much." (page 13)

Use the seven pieces of the tangram square to make the cat.

Activity: To use descriptive words to create an image

Medium

The narrator of the story relates that she is always in the same grade with Imogene Herdman, and "…what I did was stay out of her way…But if you were sort of a medium kid like me, and kept your mouth shut when the teacher said, 'Who can name all fifty states?' you had a pretty good chance to stay clear of Imogene.' " (page 8)

What other things can you think of that would make a kid "medium"? Use descriptive words to create a word picture of a "medium kid." Write the word picture in the space below.

A Medium Kid

_____

_____

_____

_____

_____

_____

_____

_____

_____

_____

_____

_____

_____

_____

Activity: To use the letters of one word to form others; spelling practice

The Pageant

How many words can you make from the letters in the word PAGEANT in three minutes? Compare your list of words with the list of words of another member of the group. Can you learn from one another?

PEA

TAN

_____   _____   _____

_____   _____   _____

_____   _____   _____

_____   _____   _____

_____   _____   _____

How many words can you make from the letters in the words BEST PAGEANT EVER in three minutes? Work with a partner for an additional three minutes. Can you add to your lists?

The letters are: BESTPAGEANTEVER

PAGE

RAGE

BETTER

_____   _____   _____

_____   _____   _____

_____   _____   _____

_____   _____   _____

_____   _____   _____

_____   _____

_____   _____

Activity: To make a choice; to give directions

Dessert

"For three days in a row Leroy Herdman stole the dessert from Charlie's lunch box and finally Charlie gave up trying to do anything about it." (page 21)

What is your favorite dessert? How is it made? Write out a recipe for your favorite dessert. Include directions to follow and make illustrations to go with the directions.

My Favorite Dessert:

_____

_____

_____

_____

_____

_____

_____

_____

_____

_____

_____

_____

_____

_____

_____

Name_____

Activity: Dessert word recognition, grouping of letters into words

Dessert Word Search Puzzle

Do the word search. Write down the letters that have not been used, starting at the top and working left to right in each row. Group letters into words to find out what Leroy Herdman does that bothers Charlie.

_____ from Charlie's lunchbox.

<table>
<tr><td>

Pie

APPLE
BUTTERSCOTCH
CHOCOLATE CHIFFON
BLACKBERRY
COCONUT CREAM
CARAMEL CUSTARD
PUMPKIN
LEMON MERINGUE
DATE
NUT
GRAPE
</td><td>

```
C  H  O  C  O  L  A  T  E  C  H  I  F  F  O  N
O  A  N  U  T  A  P  P  L  E  S  A  U  C  E  P
C  B  R  H  E  Y  D  F  S  P  O  I  T  O  B  U
O  E  L  A  S  E  A  R  U  U  U  C  U  O  U  D
N  R  C  A  M  R  T  U  G  M  R  E  R  K  T  D
U  W  A  L  C  E  E  I  A  P  C  C  N  I  T  I
T  T  H  N  A  K  L  T  R  K  R  R  O  E  E  N
C  E  A  I  G  I  B  C  L  I  E  E  V  S  R  G
R  S  T  H  T  E  R  E  U  N  A  A  E  G  S  Y
E  T  O  R  T  E  S  S  R  S  M  M  R  R  C  O
A  E  D  E  A  P  P  L  E  R  T  S  S  A  O  G
M  A  R  B  L  E  I  S  E  R  Y  A  T  P  T  U
G  R  A  H  A  M  C  R  A  C  K  E  R  E  C  R
L  E  M  O  N  M  E  R  I  N  G  U  E  D  H  T
```
</td></tr>
</table>

Cake

TORTE
SUGAR
GRAHAM CRACKER
SOUR CREAM
APPLESAUCE
WHITE
SPICE
MARBLE
ORANGE
LAYER

Other

ICE CREAM   ECLAIRS
PUDDING   FRUIT
TURNOVERS   COOKIES
YOGURT

Activity: To use mathematics skills

A Present

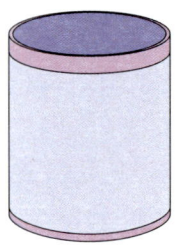

" 'Where do you get the cake?' Ralph asked the Sunday school superintendent, and Mr. Grady said, 'Well, son, I don't know about any cake, but they're collecting the food packages out in the kitchen.' What he meant was the canned stuff we brought in every year as a Thanksgiving present for the Orphans Home." (page 22)

Help to make a collection of canned and packaged dry food for the food depository in your area. Because of the manner in which food items are currently priced, local food ads may be used for this activity.

List suitable items, giving the weight and price of each. Calculate cost per ounce, rounding up to nearest cent. (Prices used below are current for March, 1995.) Calculate the price per ounce for the items listed below, and add them to the chart.

Item	Quantity	Weight Each	Price (total)	Price/Ounce rounded up to next cent
Rice-A-Roni®	2	4.3 oz.	$1.50	
Stove Top Stuffing®	1	6 oz.	79¢	_____
Canned mushrooms	5	4 oz.	$2.00	_____
Peanut Butter	1	18 oz.	99¢	_____
Star Kist® Tuna	4	6 oz.	$2.00	_____
Rice Krispies®	1	15 oz.	$1.69	_____
Pasta	2	32 oz.	$1.00	_____
Corn Flakes	1	18 oz.	99¢	_____
Instant Oatmeal	1	11.8 oz.	$1.54	_____
Potato Buds®	1	13.75	$1.07	_____
				_____

Activity: To use mathematics skills, continued

The greatest concentration in poverty is among children, and with that has come increased hunger. Think of other ways that you may help the situation in your area.

What if you decided to donate money to your local food bank, and set aside 2¢ every time you ate a meal or a snack? **Place a tally mark on a sheet of paper for every time you eat.** How much money would you have in a week? a month? a year?

What if you were able to collect and donate the coupon and special ad savings from one trip to the grocery store? How much money would that be? (The coupon amount discounted is usually listed at the bottom of the grocery store receipt.)

For this activity, use the ad from the local grocery store that lists the specials and savings for a specific amount of time. Record the items and savings for products that are normally used in your household. If you are also able to borrow product coupons from others for the items listed, add that amount to your record.

Calculate the amount of savings for the items listed below. Make your own record, and calculate the savings for the products listed.

Item	Original Cost	Sale Price	Amount Saved	Amount of coupon	Sale Savings plus coupon = total savings
Corn Flakes	$1.99	99¢	_____	25¢	_____
Salad Dressing	$2.85	$1.42	_____	35¢	_____
Candy Bar	$1.49	74¢	_____	30¢	_____
Hot Dog Buns	$1.29	64¢	_____	none	_____
Pancake Syrup	$2.69	$1.99	_____	none	_____
Pancake Mix	$1.49	$1.29	_____	none	_____
Grapefruit Juice	$2.69	$1.99	_____	25¢	_____

TOTAL: _____

Activity: To learn some food facts

Refreshments

"It was just our bad luck that the Herdmans picked that Sunday to come, because when they saw all the cans of spaghetti and beans and grape drink and peanut butter, they figured there might be some truth to what Charlie said about refreshments." (page 22)

Food is crucial as a fuel for the body. Match up the food fact question to its corresponding answer by drawing a line from the question to the answer. Learn as you are doing it.

Food Fact Questions	Answers
1. On an ordinary sort of warmish day, how much of the food you eat goes to maintain your body temperature?	a) All of these dishes were invented in the United States.
2. About how many pounds of food does the average American eat in a year? (500 pounds, 1,500 pounds, 5,000 pounds, 8,500 pounds)	b) About half of the people get enough to eat. The rest of the people on earth are hungry, malnourished, or starving.
3. What U.S. state is famous for its potatoes?	c) On an ordinary day, one half of the food intake is used to maintain body temperature.
	d) Idaho
4. The average human body needs 2,500 calories per day to maintain itself. What portion of humanity gets this many?	e) The average American consumes about 1,425 pounds of food per year, according to the USDA.
5. Name the country of origin of the following dishes: Chop Suey, Swiss Steak, Hamburger in a bun, Russian Dressing.	

What is your favorite food? Why? Do you know something about the origin of this food? Find out an interesting fact about it, and share your information with others.

_____

_____

_____

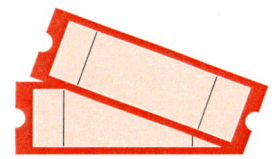

Activity: To use mathematics skills

Moviegoers

"All of the Herdmans are big moviegoers, though they never pay their own way." (page 23)

Get the movie section from the newspaper, and make a survey of the prices charged by the theaters near you. Make a graph of the information. Compute the price of admission for the six Herdman children at each price. Please put information on the back of this page. Thank you.

The following information is from the *Daily Herald* Newspaper, Arlington Heights, Illinois, March 10,1995.

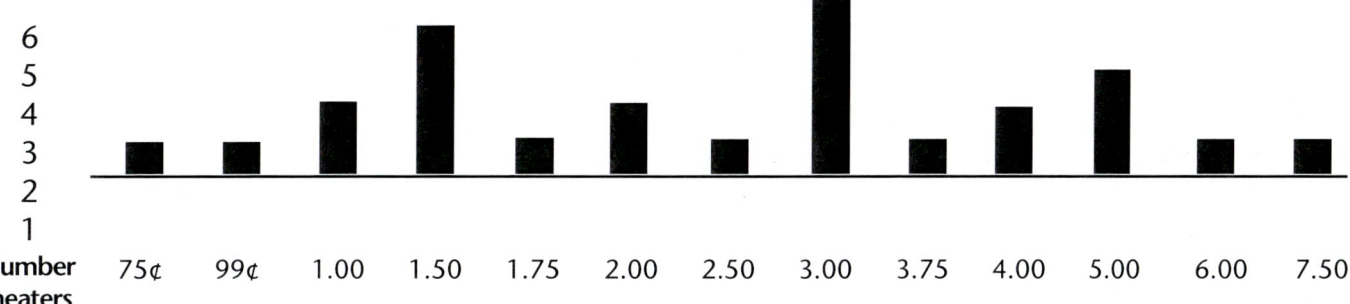

Write a summary statement about the graph above, and about your own graph, that follows. (What is the highest price in the survey? ...the lowest price? What is the price most often charged?) Please use back of page for your summary statements.

My Survey Graph

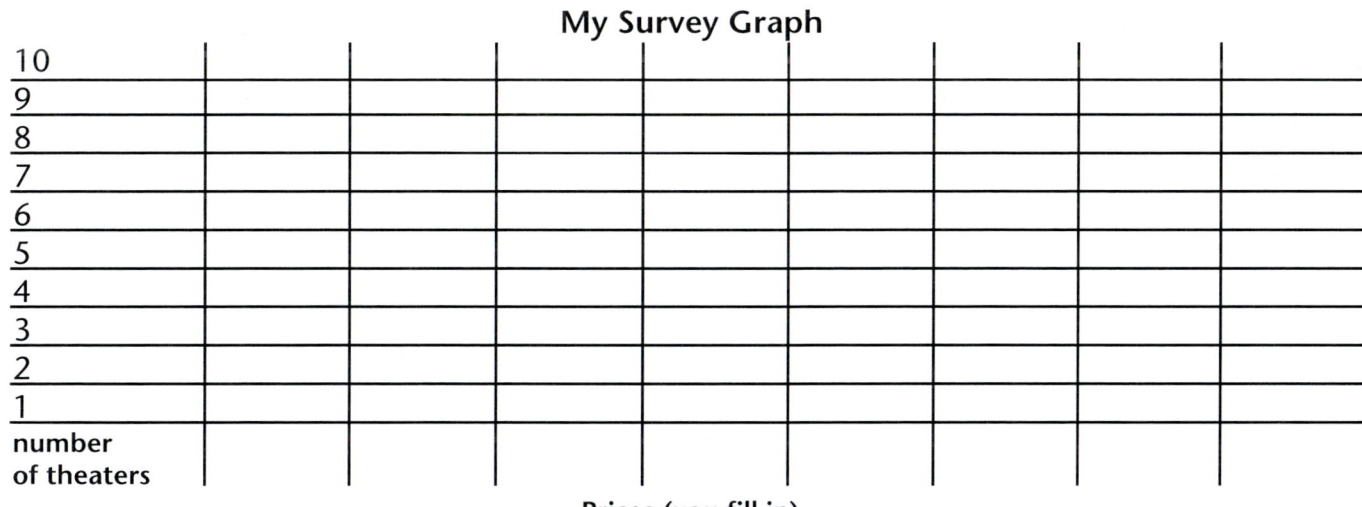

Prices (you fill in)

_____

Name_____

Activity: To use visual perceptual skills

Tangram Shepherd

"The older boys and girls will be shepherds and guests at the inn and members of the choir."
(page 28)

Use the seven pieces of the tangram square to make the shepherd.

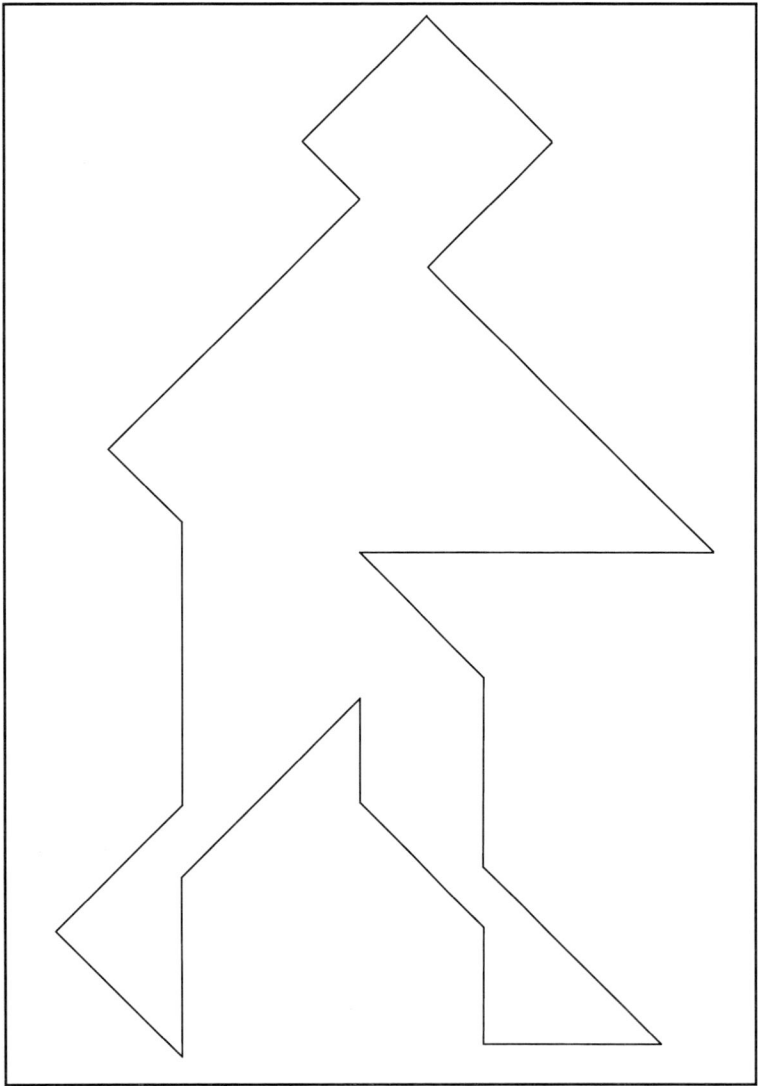
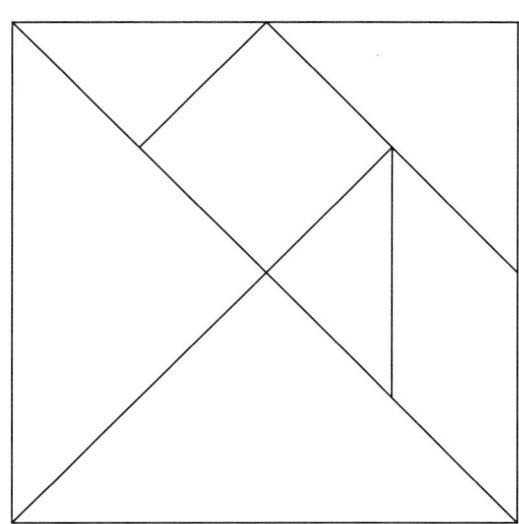

Name_____

Activity: To use visual perceptual skills, continued

Tangram
Guest At The Inn

Use the seven pieces of the tangram square to make the lady guest at the inn.

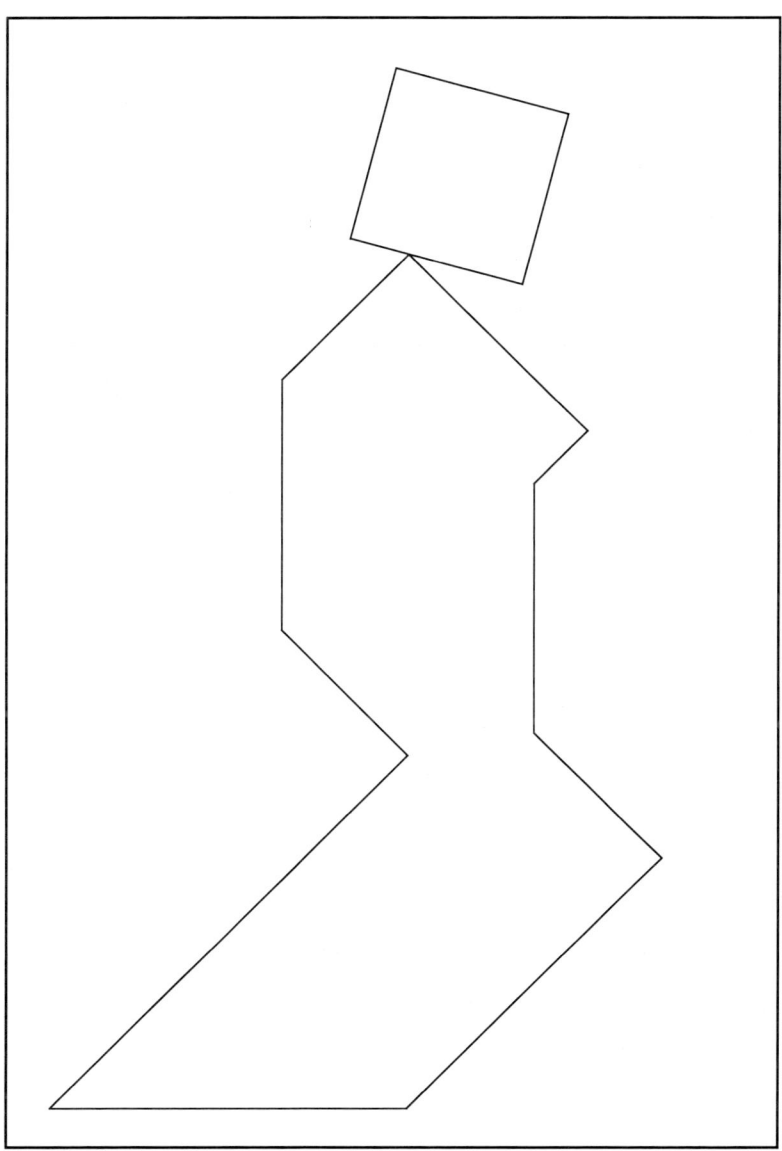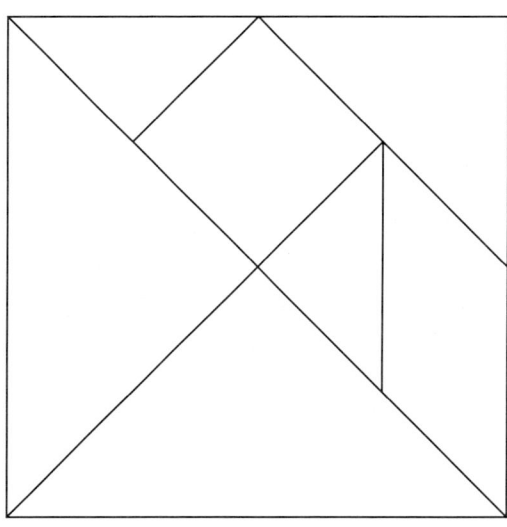

Activity: To follow directions

A Dough Character

Object: to make a pageant character

Materials:
1 1/2 cups flour
3/4 cup salt
3/4 cup water
bowl
newspaper
measuring cup

Process:

a) Cover the work area with newspaper.
b) Mix all ingredients in the bowl.
c) Add more water if needed.
d) Use your hands to knead ingredients into a soft dough.
e) Model as with any dough.
f) Place in drying area.
g) Clean up the work area.

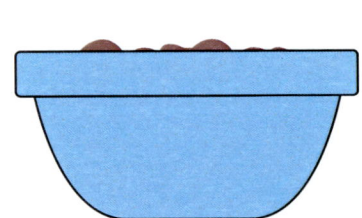

Activity: To make a choice; to explain the rules

Televised Sports

"…and all the fathers wanted to go home and watch the football game on TV." (p.29)

Choose a sporting event that you would watch on television, even though it may not be your favorite thing to do. To the best of your knowledge, write an explanation of the sport and its rules. This may be done as a serious report, or as a humorous view of the event. Illustrate your work on a separate sheet of paper.

Sporting Event: _____

Reporter: _____

_____

_____

_____

_____

_____

_____

_____

_____

_____

_____

_____

_____

_____

_____

_____

_____

_____

_____

_____

_____

Activity: To follow directions

Flat Paper Chain

"I'm going to make this the very best Christmas pageant anybody ever saw..." (p. 37)

Object: To make flat paper chains for decoration.

Materials:
colored paper
scissors
pattern for circle 2-3/4 inches in diameter, with center cut out

Process:
1. Make a pattern for a circle 2-3/4 inches in diameter, with center cut out.
2. Fold paper and cut double circle on fold.
3. To make chain, loop one circle through another and continue looping each new circle through the proceeding one.

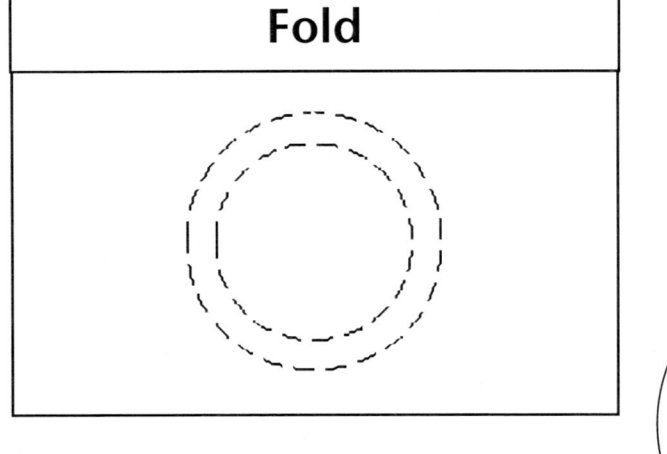

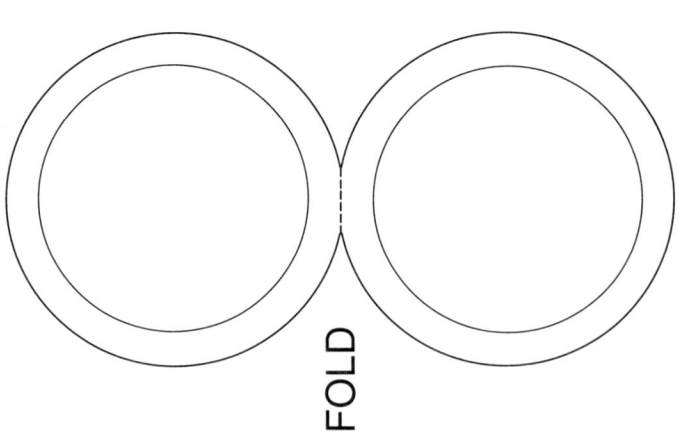

Activity: To relate the past to the present time

No Place To Stay

"...and when Mother read about there being no room at the inn, Imogene's jaw dropped and she sat up in her seat." (page 43)

The National Coalition for the Homeless reports that there are more homeless people now than in any other period of history.

Think about the people in the story that Mother is reading to the group of children, of the homeless people in the area in which you live, and of how you might feel if you had no special place to go at the end of the day.

Express your feelings by adding on to the following poem, or by writing a poem of your own.

Ladybird, ladybird, fly away home!
The Mother Goose rhyme has to say.
But what if there is no home;
No place for a person to stay?

Activity: To think creatively

No Bed

" 'What would you do if you had a new baby and no bed to put the baby in?'
'We put Gladys in a bureau drawer,' Imogene volunteered." (page 43)

What else might be used in your household as a bed for a baby?

_____

_____

_____

_____

What alternatives do you have if, for some reason, you could not use your bed tonight?
(List at least three.)

1. _____

   _____

2. _____

   _____

3. _____

   _____

4. _____

   _____

Which of these alternatives would you choose? Why?

_____

_____

_____

_____

_____

_____

_____

Activity: To make a comparison

Swaddling Clothes

" 'Swaddling clothes.' Mother sighed. 'Long ago, people used to wrap their babies very tightly in big pieces of material, so they couldn't move around. It made the babies feel cozy and comfortable.' I thought it probably just made the babies mad." (p. 44)

In addition to restricting the movement of the baby, what other reasons might there be for wrapping a baby in swaddling clothes?

_____

_____

_____

_____

_____

Current Infant Clothing: Make a list of clothes that a baby would wear. (If necessary, look in catalogs, newspapers and magazines for ideas.)

_____

_____

_____

_____

_____

_____

What was your favorite outfit or item of clothing when you were very young? Please describe it.

_____

_____

_____

_____

_____

_____

© Novel Units, Inc.

Activity: To set a priority

One Gift

"Sometimes the Herdmans got Christmas presents at the Firemen's Party, but the Santa Claus always had to feel all around the packages to be sure they weren't getting bows and arrows or dart guns or anything like that. Imogene usually got sewing cards or jigsaw puzzles and she never liked them, but I guess she figured they were better than oil."
(page 46)

Object of Activity: Think of a gift to give one of the Herdman children.

First, determine the grade level of each child, so that you will have an idea of what would be an appropriate gift. You have these clues and the one next to Claude's name:

Clue #1: "The Herdmans moved from grade to grade in school. They never got kept back. There was always another Herdman coming along, and no teacher wanted two of them at the same time."

Clue #2: The names of the children are listed from oldest to youngest, Ralph being the oldest.

Put grade level beside name.

Ralph: _____
Imogene: _____
Leroy: _____
Claude: _____ "One day Claude Herdman emptied the whole first grade in three minutes…"
Ollie: _____
Gladys: _____

Name of child to receive gift: _____

Gift: _____

Reason for choice of gift: _____

Name_____

Activity: Vocabulary word recognition, grouping of letters into words, and word usage

Vocabulary Word Search Puzzle

Do the word search. Write down the letters that have not been used, starting at the top and working left to right in each row. Group letters into words to find out the part that the Herdmans have in the pageant.

The Herdmans _____.

```
B  E  W  I  L  D  E  R  E  D
A  C  O  N  F  E  R  O  P  M
R  O  A  L  U  C  K  L  I  Y
K  L  H  S  A  P  V  E  P  R
E  I  E  T  H  O  E  E  R
D  C  S  C  R  I  P  T  D  H
L  E  I  N  S  A  N  E  A  D
P  E  W  S  M  A  N  G  E  R
```

BEWILDERED
INSANE
MYRRH
COLIC
LUCK
BARKED
MANGER
ROLE
PEW
POT
CASTING
SCRIPT
CONFER
PIPED

Some other things to do:

1. Put the words in alphabetical order.
2. Define half of the words.
3. Use the remaining half of the words in sentences.

Activity: To keep a record

...Write It Down

"One day I saw Alice Wendleken writing something down on a little pad of paper, and trying to hide it with her other hand." (page 54)

Alice is keeping a record of "just how awful" the Herdmans are being.

Keep a record of how many times you do something nice in a day, such as smile, help someone, greet someone with a "hi" or "hello," etc., and where you are when you do it. Make some conclusions at the end of the day. (Do you smile enough, etc.?)

Smile	*Help Someone*

Greet Someone	*Other*

Activity: To follow directions

Decorations

Object of Activity: To make decorations for the room, home, a project, and/or for fun.

Materials: strips of colored paper, scissors, glue, small stapler and staples, newspaper

Process:
1. Cover the work area with newspaper.
2. Place the materials on the newspaper.
3. Make loops and rings with the strips of paper, gluing or stapling the ends together.
4. Position loops and rings into a pleasing design.
5. Staple the design together to hold in place.
6. Create more original designs.
7. Clean up the work area.

Variations:
  a) Use ribbon instead of paper.
  b) Dot glue on paper/ribbon and sprinkle with glitter.
  c) Make a mobile out of some of the designs by stringing them together with dark thread.

Activity: To read for information

"What *did* happen to Herod, anyway?"

(page 50)

Herod was the name of a ruling family in Palestine during the 100's B.C. and the first 100 years after Christ's birth, while Palestine was part of the Roman Empire.

Herod the Great (about 73 B.C.–about 4 B.C.) ruled all of Palestine as king of Judea from 37 B.C. until his death. Throughout his reign, he put down plots against his leadership by killing anyone suspected of threatening his throne. The executions included three of his sons and several other family members.

His ruthlessness is illustrated in the story of the slaughter of the infant boys in and around Bethlehem. Herod ordered their deaths in an attempt to kill the infant Jesus.

Herod began a widespread building program in Palestine. In Jerusalem, he built a theater, a palace, rebuilt the fortress, and began rebuilding the Jewish Temple. He also built or rebuilt many other fortresses, including Masada. In addition, he constructed the seaport of Caesarea.

After Herod's death, three of his sons inherited his kingdom.

Source for Information: Information Finder, 1994 World Book, Inc.

Read the following statements. Mark each either T (True) or F (False).

_____   1.   Herod was the name of a ruling family in Palestine.

_____   2.   Herod the Great did not plot to kill those who threatened his rule.

_____   3.   Herod the Great ordered the deaths of infant boys in and around Bethlehem.

_____   4.   Herod the Great did not want to kill the infant Jesus.

_____   5.   Herod the Great had three of his sons executed.

_____   6.   Herod the Great did nothing to build up and improve Palestine.

Activity: To match vocabulary word with definition

Vocabulary Crossword Puzzle

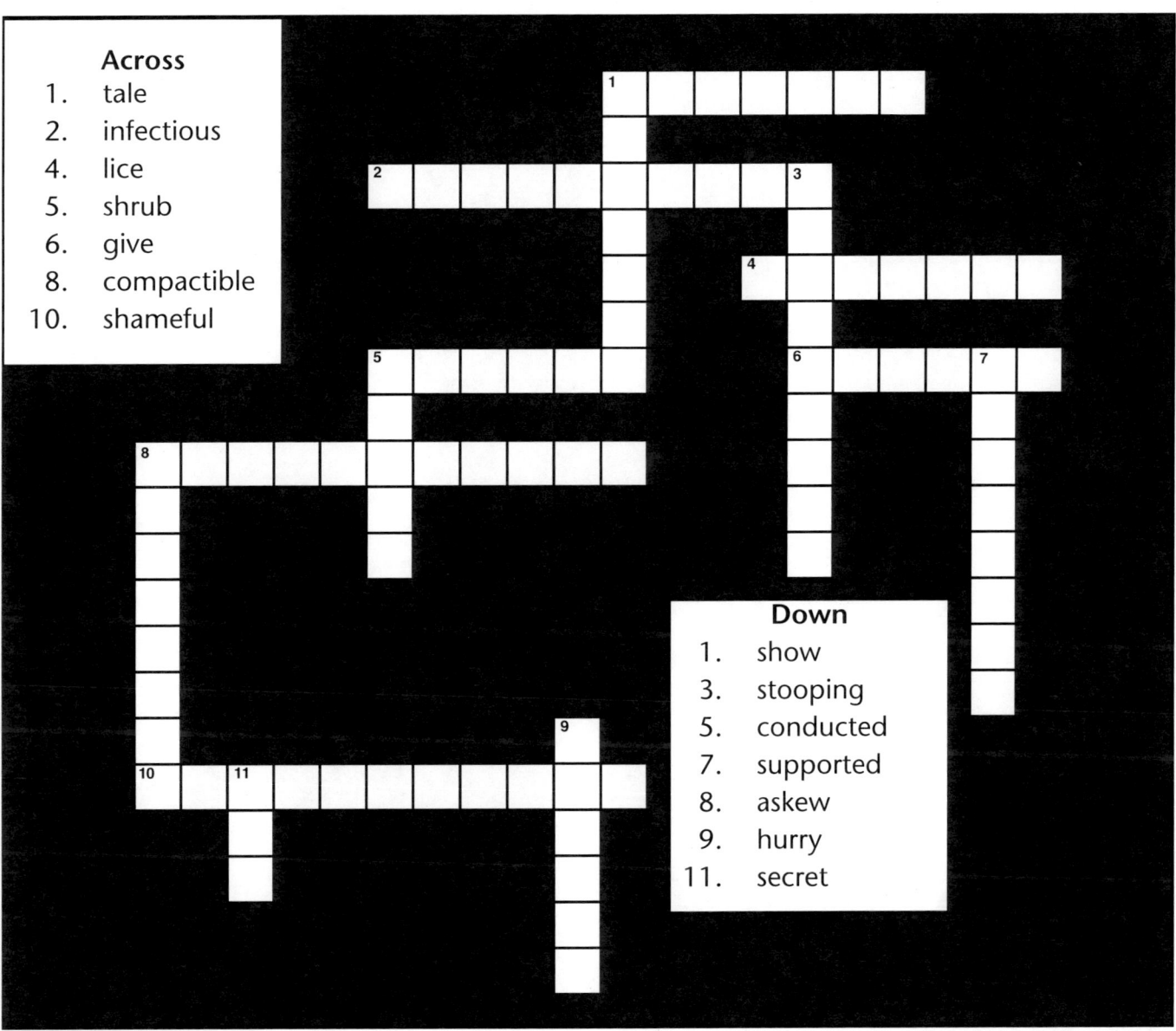

Across
1. tale
2. infectious
4. lice
5. shrub
6. give
8. compactible
10. shameful

Down
1. show
3. stooping
5. conducted
7. supported
8. askew
9. hurry
11. secret

(Vocabulary words used: cockeyed, collapsible, confer, contagious, cooties, disgraceful, espoused, hustle, pageant, parable, piped, privet, slouching, sly)

Activity: To use own knowledge in a creative manner

Lucky Pot

"Our last rehearsal happened to be the night before the pot-luck supper..." (page 60)

Use each letter in POT LUCK SUPPER, below, as the beginning letter of something that could be served to the people attending.

P _____

O _____

T _____

L _____

U _____

C _____

K _____

S _____

U _____

P _____

P _____

E _____

R _____

Which of the things on your list do you like the best?_____

Activity: To write similes

Comparisons

"There was a big crash at the back of the church, as if somebody dropped all the collection plates."
(page 65)

A **simile** suggests a similarity between two things, using words such as **like, as, than, similar to, resembles,** etc. to highlight the comparison being made.

Example: She is as bouncy as popping corn.

The following phrases are taken from Chapter 6 of *The Best Christmas Pageant Ever.* Finish each by using a **simile.**

Page 60: When we got there the kitchen was full of ladies. _____

_____

Page 61: She had even put Vaseline on her eyelids, so they would shine in the candlelight

_____

_____

Page 65: By that time everyone was hot and tired, _____

_____

Page 66: The firemen hurried in _____

_____

Page 68: She whirled around and marched back to the kitchen_____

_____

Page 69: The whole church is in an uproar _____

_____

Write your own simile: _____

_____

© Novel Units, Inc.

33

Activity: To follow directions; to be creative

Circles

"...the committee decided to come in this evening and set up the tables and all." (page 60)

Object: To make decorations

Materials: newspaper, colored paper, scissors, crayons, paste or glue, crayons and/or watercolor markers, pencil, flat objects having a circle-shape that may be used as patterns.

Process:
    a) Cover the work area with newspaper.
    b) Place the materials to be used on the newspaper.
    c) Make some colored paper circle shapes.
    d) Arrange the circle shapes in different ways, to determine what you like (shapes may be folded, slit, etc.)
    e) Cut additional shapes to complete your design.
    f) Paste or glue the shapes together.
    g) Determine use and complete.
    h) Clean up the work area.

Name_____

Activity: To make a comparison using a synonym or an antonym of a vocabulary word

Vocabulary Review

Use the following vocabulary words in this activity:

VAIN	**SACRILEGIOUS**	**SLY**
ESPOUSED	**DISGRACEFUL**	**COCKEYED**

Complete each of the following comparisons by using one of the above vocabulary words.

Sample of activity: GOOD is to BAD as HOT is to COLD.

1. MARVELOUS is to WONDERFUL as _____ is to CONCEITED.

2. BETTER is to WORSE as _____ is to PIOUS.

3. FORLORN is to HAPPY as _____ is to SINCERE.

4. SOOTHING is to AGGRAVATING as _____ is to REJECTED.

5. SCARED is to FRIGHTENED as _____ is to SHAMEFUL.

6. PITIFUL is to PATHETIC as _____ is to ASKEW.

Make up two of your own comparisons. You do not have to use vocabulary words.

a) _____

_____

b) _____

_____

Name_____

Activity: To use thinking skills to make choices

Hamburgers

" 'When it's all over,' he [father] said, 'we'll go someplace and have hamburgers.' " (page 70)

What will you have on your hamburger? Here are the choices:

cheese (CH)   lettuce (L)   tomato (T)   mustard (M)
pickles (P)   catsup (C)   onion (O)

How many **different** combinations, using two or more of the above choices, can you think of for your hamburger? (Use the letters as word substitutes.)

cheese and lettuce (CH & L)   _____   _____

lettuce and tomato (L & T)   _____   _____

_____   _____   _____

_____   _____   _____

_____   _____   _____

_____   _____

_____   _____

_____   _____

_____   _____

_____   _____

Briefly summarize the story, and write about the thoughts, feelings and questions that you had as the story ended.

_____

_____

_____

_____

_____

_____

_____

_____

_____

_____

_____

_____

_____

_____

_____

_____

_____

_____

_____

_____

_____

_____

_____

_____

_____

To The Teacher:

The concluding activity may be used as the final test for the novel unit.

The student is asked to summarize the story, and to write about the thoughts, feelings and questions that remained after the story ended.

Any of the following pages may be used as quiz pages if the teacher so desires.

a) Prereading Activity, Worksheet #1, Special Trees. To read for information.

b) Chapter 2, Worksheet #9, The Pageant. To use the letters of one word to form others; spelling practice.

c) Chapter 2, Worksheet #11, Dessert Word Search Puzzle. Dessert word recognition; grouping of letters into words.

d) Chapter 3, Worksheet #19, Flat Paper Chain. To follow directions.

e) Chapter 5, Worksheet #24, Vocabulary Word Search Puzzle. Vocabulary word recognition, grouping of letters into words, and word usage.

f) Chapter 5, Worksheet #27, "What *did* happen to Herod, anyway?" To read for information.

g) Chapter 6, Worksheet #28, Vocabulary Crossword Puzzle. To match vocabulary word with definition.

h) Chapter 7, Worksheet #32, Vocabulary Review. To make a comparison using a synonym or an antonym of a vocabulary word.

Quiz for comprehension follows.

Read the following information. Fill in the blank space in each with a word, words or phrase that will make the information given complete and true to the story.

Sample: The name of this novel is *(The Best Christmas Pageant Ever).*

1. _____ were the worst kids in the world.

2. The Herdmans learn that wherever there is a fire there will be free _____ sooner or later.

3. Mrs. Herdman walks the _____ on a length of chain.

4. The Herdmans go to Sunday School to get some free _____.

5. The pageant has all of the Herdmans in the main _____.

6. The Herdmans are so interested in the pageant's story, they go to the _____ to get information.

7. Imogene offers to steal a _____ at the supermarket.

8. Everybody says that the pageant is the _____ ever, but they don't know _____.

Answers

Worksheet #1

1. TRUE
2. FALSE
3. TRUE
4. TRUE
5. FALSE
6. TRUE

Worksheet #3

The Herdmans would each get 10 donuts.

Jewel	1	39¢	39¢	$ 4.68
7-11	10	$2.89	29¢	$ 3.48
Dunkin' Donuts	1	49¢	49¢	$ 5.88
Patisserie	6	$6.99	$1.17	$14.04
Cake Box	1	65¢	65¢	$ 7.80

Worksheet #9

The Pageant   SOME WORDS FROM THE LETTERS OF THE WORD *PAGEANT* FOLLOW:

PEA	TAP	TAPE	NAP
TAN	GAP	GAPE	GNAT
TAG	PAGE	NAPE	ANT

SOME WORDS FROM *BESTPAGEANTEVER* FOLLOW:
(include all of the above)

PAGE	NEVER	STAGE	SNARE
SPAR	GET	VET	RAGE
PANT	STREET	STARE	VENT
PET	BAN	BETTER	RANT
STEP	STAR	VAN	NET
GAVE			

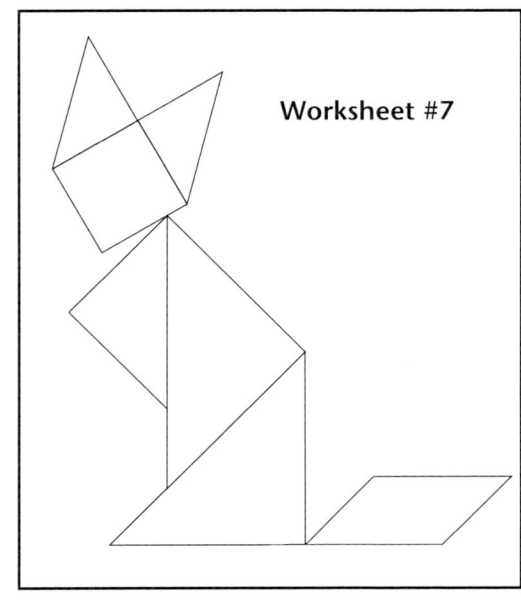

Worksheet #7

Worksheet #12

Item	Quantity	Weight Each	Price (total)	Price/Ounce (rounded up to next cent)
Rice-A-Roni®	2	4.3 oz.	$1.50	18¢
Stove Top Stuffing®	1	6 oz.	79¢	14¢
Canned mushrooms	5	4 oz.	$2.00	10¢
Peanut Butter	1	18 oz.	99¢	6¢
Starkist® Tuna	4	6 oz.	$2.00	9¢
Rice Krispies®	1	15 oz.	$1.69	12¢
Pasta	2	32 oz.	$1.00	2¢
Corn Flakes	1	18 oz.	99¢	6¢
Instant Oatmeal	1	11.8 oz.	$1.54	14¢
Potato Buds®	1	13.75	$1.07	8¢

Worksheet #12 (Answers in boldface type.)

Item	Original Cost	Sale Price	Amount Saved	Amount of coupon	Sale Savings plus coupon = total savings
Corn Flakes	$1.99	99¢	**$1.00**	25¢	**$1.25**
Salad Dressing	$2.85	$1.42	**$1.43**	35¢	**$1.78**
Candy Bar	$1.49	74¢	**75¢**	30¢	**$1.05**
Hot Dog Buns	$1.29	64¢	**65¢**	none	**65¢**
Pancake Syrup	$2.69	$1.99	**70¢**	none	**70¢**
Pancake Mix	$1.49	$1.29	**20¢**	none	**20¢**
Grapefruit Juice	$2.69	$1.99	**70¢**	25¢	**95¢**
				TOTAL	**$6.58**

Worksheet #13
1-c
2-e
3-d
4-b
5-a

Worksheet #14
Ralph: fourth grade
Imogene: third grade
Leroy: second grade
Claude: "One day Claude Herdman emptied the whole **first grade** in three minutes..."
Ollie: kindergarten
Gladys: preschool/prekindergarten/nursery school/head start/home

Worksheet #15

Worksheet #11

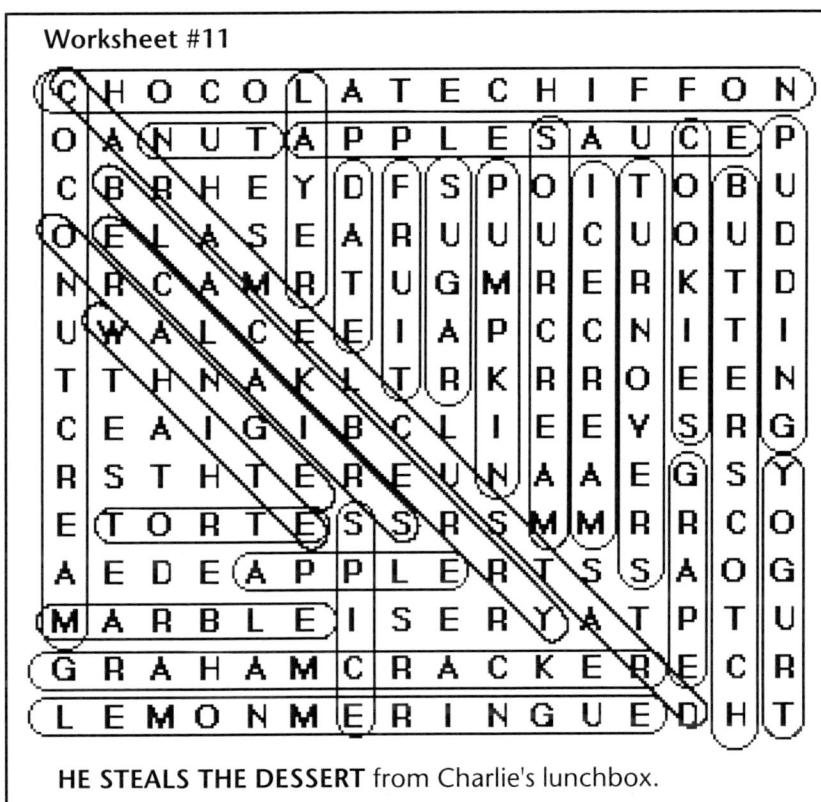

HE STEALS THE DESSERT from Charlie's lunchbox.

Worksheet #16

Worksheet #24

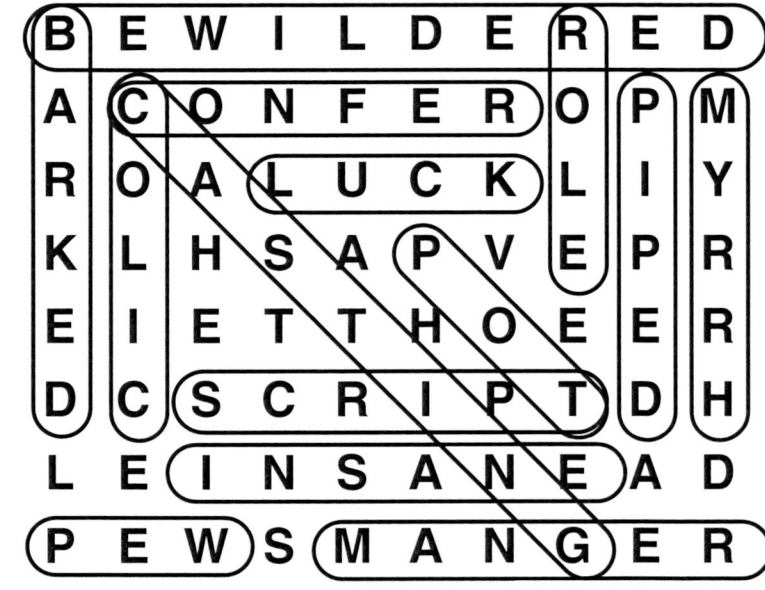

The Herdmans **HAVE THE LEADS.**

Worksheet #27

1. T
2. F
3. T
4. F
5. T
6. F

Worksheet #29
(example)
POTATOES
ONIONS
TEA
LEMON
UGLY FRUIT
CUCUMBERS
KIWI FRUIT
SALSA SAUCE
UPSIDE DOWN CAKE
PINEAPPLE
PEACHES
EGGPLANT
RADISHES

Worksheet #28

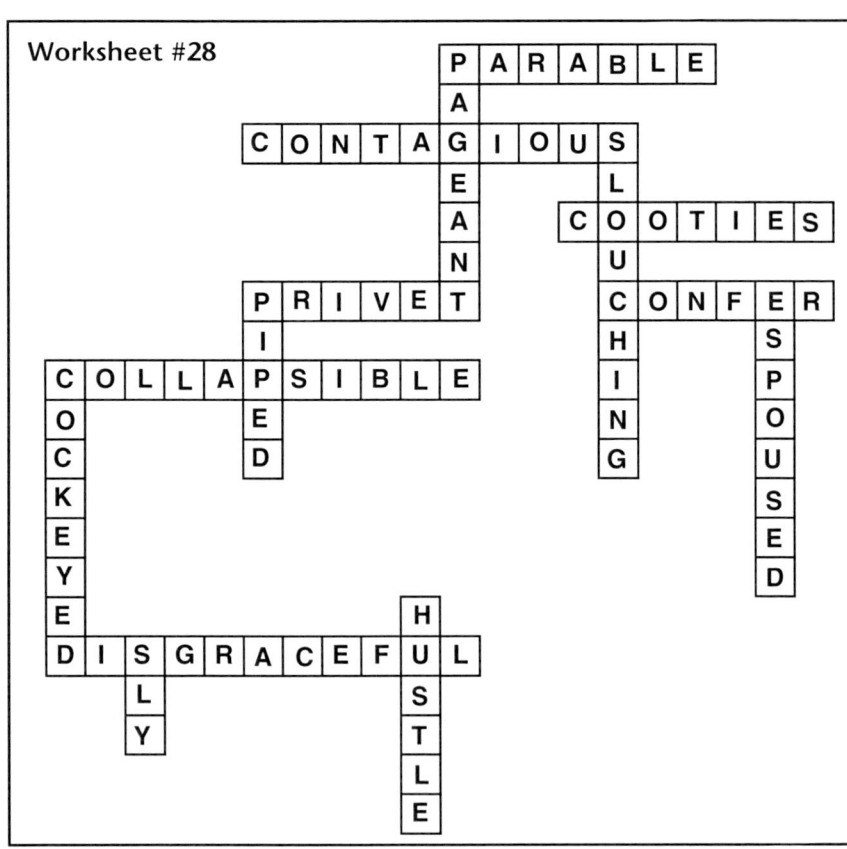

Worksheet #30
Simile examples:
Page 60: When we got there the kitchen was full of ladies **rushing around like hens at the feed.**
Page 61: She had even put Vaseline on her eyelids, so they would shine in the candlelight **like neon signs.**
Page 65: By that time everyone was hot and tired, **like leftovers microwaved too long.**
Page 66: The firemen hurried in **as fast as hounds after the fox.**
Page 68: She whirled around and marched back to the kitchen, **looking like a drum major in need of a baton.**
Page 69: The whole church is in an uproar, **resembling an earthquake about to happen.**

Worksheet #32
1. VAIN
2. SACRILEGIOUS
3. SLY
4. ESPOUSED
5. DISGRACEFUL
6. COCKEYED

Worksheet #33 (some possible combinations)

CH & L	L & M	CH & M & P	L & T & M	CH & L & T & M & P
CH & T	L & P	CH & M & C	L & T & P	CH & L & T & M & C
CH & M	L & C	CH & M & O	L &T & C	CH & L & T & M & O
CH & P	L & O	CH & P & C	L & T & O	CH & T & M & P & C
CH & C	T & M	CH & P & O	T & M & P	CH & T & M & P & O
CH & O	T & P	CH & C & O	T & M & C	CH & M & P & C & O
CH & L & T	T & C	CH & L & T & M	T & M & O	CH & L & T & M & P & C
CH & L & M	T & O	CH & L & T & P	M & P & C	CH & L & T & M & P & O
CH & L & P	M & P	CH & L & T & C	M & P & O	CH & T & M & P & C & O
CH & L & C	M & C	CH & L & T & O	P & C & O	CH & L & T & M & P & C & O
CH & L & O	M & O	CH & T & M & P	L & T & M & P	
CH & T & M	P & C	CH & T & M & C	L & T & M & C	
CH & T & P	P & O	CH & T & M & O	L & T & M & O	
CH & T & C	C & O	CH & M & P & C	M & P & C & O	
CH & T & O	L & T	CH & M & P & O	CH & P & C &O	

Quiz
1. the Herdmans
2. doughnuts
3. cat
4. food/dessert
5. roles/parts
6. library
7. baby
8. best–why

Notes: